SUN OF GOD
Know for Yourself

K. T. Hazine

© 2024 K. T. Hazine

Published by Hazine Publishing

All rights reserved. No part of this book may be reproduced, stored in a retrieval system, or transmitted in any form or by any means—electronic, mechanical, photocopying, recording, or otherwise—without prior written permission of the copyright holder, except for brief quotations embodied in critical reviews and certain other non-commercial uses permitted by copyright law.

For permissions requests or inquiries, please contact hazinepublishing@editorschair.com

ISBN: 978-1-0686564-0-8

Editorial Production: The Editor's Chair

Printed in United Kingdom

In Loving Memory of My Late Father, N.N.G. Lewis

Note from the Author:

As the daughter of a pastor and having studied Theology for several years, I naturally sought to follow in the footsteps of my beloved father. However, the journey to this path was not straightforward; it led me to question my faith, knowledge, and the discoveries I encountered.

Through countless late nights and early mornings of study, I have gathered morsels of information and captured striking images to illustrate my findings. While this information may not resonate with everyone, the mantra remains: "Know for yourself."

K. T. Hazine

Table of contents

01 INTRODUCTION ~~~~~~~~~~~~~~~~~~~~~~~~ 7
02 26 WAYS OF DEFINING WORDS: ~~~~~~~~~~~ 9
03 GOD'S SUN ~~~~~~~~~~~~~~~~~~~~~~~~~~~ 10
04 THE STARS AND MOON ~~~~~~~~~~~~~~~~~ 12
05 TWELVE MONTHS, FOUR SEASONS ~~~~~~~~ 14
06 THE FIRST RAINS ~~~~~~~~~~~~~~~~~~~~~~ 16
07 THE WATER BEARER ~~~~~~~~~~~~~~~~~~~ 18
08 ETYMOLOGY OF THE SEVEN DAYS OF THE WEEK ~~~~ 19
09 SUNRISE ~~~~~~~~~~~~~~~~~~~~~~~~~~~~~ 20
10 ANCIENT GOD HORUS – MYTHOLOGY ~~~~~~ 22
11 SUNSET – DARKNESS ~~~~~~~~~~~~~~~~~~~ 24
12 BAPHOMET ~~~~~~~~~~~~~~~~~~~~~~~~~~~ 26
13 THE STORY OF HORUS ~~~~~~~~~~~~~~~~~~ 30
14 WORSHIP OF THE SUN/SON – BLACK MADONNA AND CHILD ~~~~~~~~~~~~~~~~~~~~~~~~~~~ 31
15 LIST OF THE OTHER GODS ~~~~~~~~~~~~~~~ 33
16 OTHER GODS! ~~~~~~~~~~~~~~~~~~~~~~~~~ 35
17 THE TRUTH IS OUT THERE ~~~~~~~~~~~~~~~ 36
18 FOLLOW THE STARS ~~~~~~~~~~~~~~~~~~~~ 38
19 THE CRUX – THE CROSS ~~~~~~~~~~~~~~~~~ 40
20 VIRGO THE VIRGIN ~~~~~~~~~~~~~~~~~~~~~ 41
21 SUN AND SON ~~~~~~~~~~~~~~~~~~~~~~~~~ 45
22 12 CONSTELLATIONS ~~~~~~~~~~~~~~~~~~~~ 46
23 GALATIANS 4:24-25 ~~~~~~~~~~~~~~~~~~~~~ 47
24 WHOSE CROSS? ~~~~~~~~~~~~~~~~~~~~~~~~ 48
25 THE COUNCIL OF CHALCEDON 451 A.D ~~~~~~ 49
26 AFRICAN BONDAGE ~~~~~~~~~~~~~~~~~~~~~ 50
27 THE BIBLE ~~~~~~~~~~~~~~~~~~~~~~~~~~~~ 52
28 COLONIALISM ~~~~~~~~~~~~~~~~~~~~~~~~~ 53

#	Title	Page
29	THE SUN OF GOD	55
30	IMAGES OF JESUS ARE ALWAYS SHOWN WITH THE SUN DISK OR HALO BEHIND HIS HEAD.	57
31	THE SUN OF GOD COMES EVERY MORNING WITH A CROWN OF THORNS OR SUN RAYS ILLUMINATED IN THE BACKGROUND:	58
32	CROWN OF THORNS	59
33	TIME AND AGE	60
34	PERIOD IN TIME	61
35	VERNAL EQUINOX	62
36	AGES OF THE BULL, AGE OF THE RAM	63
37	THE AGE OF THE TWO FISHES AND AQUARIUS	64
38	MOSES = THE AGE OF ARIES (2150 BC - 1 AD)	65
39	THUTMOSE III	67
40	JESUS = THE AGE OF PISCES (1 AD - 2150 AD)	68
41	LAW GIVERS THROUGH THE AGES	69
42	MANU, LAW-GIVER OF INDIA	70
43	MINOS, LAW-GIVER OF CRETE	71
44	MISES, LAW-GIVER OF SYRIA	72
45	SACRIFICES ARE MADE TO SYMBOLISE THE USHERING OF A NEW AGE	73
46	SACRIFICED/CRUCIFIED	75
47	THE COUNCIL OF NICAEA 325 A.D	76
48	HORUS = JESUS	78
49	SON WORSHIP OR SUN WORSHIP	79
50	ALMIGHTY POWER	80
51	SEEK TRUTH IF YOU DARE	81
52	HISTORIANS	82
53	FLAVIUS JOSEPHUS	83
54	ANCIENT EGYPT: THE ORIGINAL BLUEPRINT OF:	84
55	LAWRENCE H. SCHIFFMAN	85
56	THIS IS A COLLECTION OF AUTHORS FOR FURTHER RESEARCH:	86

Introduction

This work is in no way a means to convince, convict, or reprove anyone. It is only a collection of information I have studied in the hope of knowing the truth, that I might not perish for lack of knowledge. Therefore, I have included as much basic information as possible in the hope that the reader will seek God in this matter and inquire to do their research. Every person should study for themselves and not solely rely on another person's understanding of the 'Word of your Bible'. The Holy Spirit is there to teach us the truth, but we must make ourselves open, teachable, and available.

Anyone can obtain knowledge; however, revelation is only given through the Holy Spirit. We must seek, therefore, for revelation and understanding. Be prepared to undo all that you thought you knew. Only then can you receive it. A time is coming when God's truth will be revealed to mankind, but what will man do with it? We pray and ask for the courage to do what are the commands of God and not the traditions of men.

It is at this point I must stress my desire to those of you who are reading or hearing this: it is not by chance that you are witnessing this revelation. Ask the Holy Spirit to open your understanding. Have we only skimmed the outline of the Bible and believe we know it, or have we completely missed the mark?

This insight forms part of my research material for my PhD. I kindly request that you refrain from condemning this perspective until you have undertaken comprehensive research. Utilising the Bible alone as a basis for justification is inadequate. It is crucial to delve into history, uncover historical facts, and maintain an impartial stance. I welcome your contributions and findings as part of my ongoing studies. If you require further material on this subject, please do not hesitate to contact me.

Thank you, Ase'.

26 Ways of Defining Words:

1. Derivative Definition
2. Translational Definition
3. Recommended Definition
4. Synonymic Definition
5. Antonymic Definition
6. Metronymic Definition
7. Classificatory Definition
8. Operational Definition
9. Description Definition
10. Historical Definition
11. Anatomic Definition
12. Qualitative Definition
13. Quantitative Definition
14. Illustrative Definition
15. Quotation Definition
16. Analogical Definition
17. Obsolescent versus Obsolete
18. Archaic Definition
19. Binomial and Phrasal
20. Ocular Definition
21. Pictorial Definition of Particulars
22. Diagram Definition of Universals
23. Aural Definition
24. Tactile Definition
25. Palatal Definition
26. Olfactoral Definition

GOD'S SUN

As far back as ten thousand B.C., history is replete with writings and carvings that venerate the Sun. The Sun was adored because, each morning, it would rise, bringing light, warmth, and energy, rescuing humanity from the cold, the stagnation of nature, and the grip of darkness. People understood the Sun's paramount significance, recognising that life itself depended on it. Indeed, the Sun held the highest place in their adoration.

THE STARS AND MOON

The stars, too, found meticulous documentation. Early civilisations grasped the stars' connection to daily life, as they influenced crop planting, seasonal transitions, eclipses, and the timing of full moons.

TWELVE MONTHS, FOUR SEASONS

This is also where we get the term "constellation" from, or the "cross of the zodiac". It is a representation of all the signs and the tracking of the movement of the Sun through the twelve major constellations over a year, reflecting also the twelve months, the four seasons, and equinoxes.

THE FIRST RAINS

The term "zodiac" basically means that the constellations were given names according to what that particular month or season brought with it. For example, the sign Aquarius is commonly known as the water bearer, as this is the time of the spring rains and so on. These names are myths made up to tell a story.

THE WATER BEARER

Etymology of the seven days of the week

Latin	Translation	Modern English
Solis dies	Day of the Sun	Sunday
Lunae dies	Day of the Moon	Monday
Martis dies	Day of Mars	Tuesday
Mercurii dies	Day of Mercury	Wednesday
Jovis dies	Day of Jupiter	Thursday
Veneris dies	Day of Venus	Friday
Saturni dies	Day of Saturn	Saturday

SUNRISE

So we have it, early civilisations wrote myths for all seasons of the zodiac. The Sun was personified as the unseen creator, giver of life, or God's Sun – "The Sun of righteousness will appear with healing in His wings" – because that is what the Sun does! It appears every morning and heals.

The Sun is said to be the light of the world, the Saviour of mankind. The attributes of the Sun represent the life force that it gives. Every morning, it would win the war against Horus (hours), which we call sunset, but every morning, Horus would rise again.

ANCIENT GOD HORUS – MYTHOLOGY

In the annals of Ancient History, the Sun received worship in the form of the Egyptian God Horus around 3000 B.C. Horus's life was portrayed as an allegory, a testament to the celestial dance around the Sun in the sky. Ancient cryptograms in Egypt unveiled the allegories of Horus's existence.

SUNSET – DARKNESS

For example, Horus had a nemesis, 'Set', also known as Sunset, Darkness, and Satan. Allegorically, Set won the battle each night, signifying sunrise.

It's crucial to remember that these are allegorical myths, embodying the eternal struggle of good versus evil, light versus darkness, a dualism that continues to resonate across various levels of human understanding today.

BAPHOMET

Traditionally known as the Devil, Baphomet is, in fact, a name with intriguing origins. It is derived from the Templar Baphomet, composed of three abbreviations: Tem.ohp.AB, which stands for "*Templi omnium hominum pacts abbas*", meaning "The Father of the temple of peace of all men", or alternatively, "The Father of understanding" (Arabic-Abu Fihama(t)).

Dr. Hugh Schonfield, renowned for his work on the Dead Sea Scrolls, proposed an interesting theory about Baphomet. Schonfield had studied a Jewish cipher called the Atbash cipher, used in translating some of the Dead Sea Scrolls. He claimed that when this cipher was applied to the word Baphomet, it transposed into the Greek word "Sophia", signifying "knowledge" and synonymous with "goddess".

The symbolism associated with Baphomet is rich and complex:

⌘ The goat depicted on the frontispiece bears a pentagram on its forehead, with one point at the top, symbolising light. Its two hands form the sign of Hermeticism, one pointing upwards to the white moon of Chesed and the other pointing down to the black moon of Geburah. This sign represents the perfect harmony of mercy and justice. One arm is female, while the other is male, aligning with the androgynous nature of Khunrath. These attributes merge because they symbolise the same concept.

⌘ The flame of intelligence shining between the goat's horns represents the magical light of universal balance. It signifies the soul elevated above matter, as the flame, though connected to matter, shines beyond it.

- ⌘ The beast's head, with its grotesque appearance, conveys the horror experienced by the sinner. The sinner's material actions, the sole cause of punishment, are represented, as the soul is, by nature, insensitive and can only suffer when it becomes materialised.

- ⌘ The rod in place of the genitals symbolises eternal life. The body adorned with scales represents water, the semi-circle above it signifies the atmosphere, and the feathers above represent the volatile.

- ⌘ Humanity is symbolised by the two breasts and the androgynous arms of this enigmatic figure, which embodies the mysteries of occult sciences.

THE STORY OF HORUS

- Horus was born on December 25th.
- Born of a virgin named Isis or Mary.
- His birth was marked by a star in the east.
- Three kings followed the star to locate and honour the newborn king and saviour, bringing gifts with them.
- At the age of twelve, Horus was a prodigious child teacher.
- At the age of thirty, he was initiated into ministry by a figure named Anap.
- Horus had twelve disciples who accompanied him as he performed acts of benevolence, such as healing the sick, raising the dead, and walking on water.
- After being betrayed by Tyfon, Horus underwent a crucifixion and remained dead for three days, only to then experience a resurrection or rebirth.

WORSHIP OF THE SUN/SON – BLACK MADONNA AND CHILD

Horus was known by many other names, including the truth, the light of the world, the lamb of God, the saviour of the world, the good shepherd, and The Sun of God, among others.

These characteristics are not unique to Horus, the Egyptian God, but are also associated with up to twenty-one other deities from various cultures worldwide.

Notably, these divine figures predate the birth of Jesus Christ, with Jesus being regarded as the final Messiah in this lineage.

LIST OF THE OTHER GODS

List of some of the other gods with similar attributes:

- Attis of Greece (1200 B.C.)
- Krishna of India (900 B.C.)
- Dionysus of Greece (500 B.C.)
- Mithra of Persia (1200 B.C.)
- Chrishna of Hindostan
- Buddha Sakia of India
- Zoroaster of Persia

- Baal & Taut – begotten god of Phoenicia
- Indra of Tibet
- Bali of Afghanistan
- Jao of Nepal
- Adad of Assyria
- Hesus or Eros of the Druids
- Ixion and Quirinus of Rome

And many more.

Research indicates the existence of up to twenty other gods with identical attributes. This apparent lack of coincidence underscores the importance of thorough historical investigation. Reading the book *The Sixteen Crucified Saviours* by Kersey Groves can shed further light on this topic.

OTHER GODS!

THE TRUTH IS OUT THERE

Through research, it becomes apparent that the human form of "Jesus Christ" was constructed through the coronation of Serapis Christos and the decisions of the Council of Nicaea in 325 A.D. Consequently, it is evident that the Bible is built on allegorical foundations.

The birth narratives of Horus, Jesus, and other gods are fundamentally astrological. It is the Story of the Sun, and not the worship of the elements, animals or nature as gods, which is what we are made to believe.

FOLLOW THE STARS

The star in the east, Sirius, the brightest star in the night sky, aligns with the three brightest stars in the Orion belt on December 24th, known as the "Three Kings". This alignment, along with Sirius, directs attention to the sunrise on December 25th, symbolising the birth of the Sun of God during the winter solstice.

THE CRUX – THE CROSS

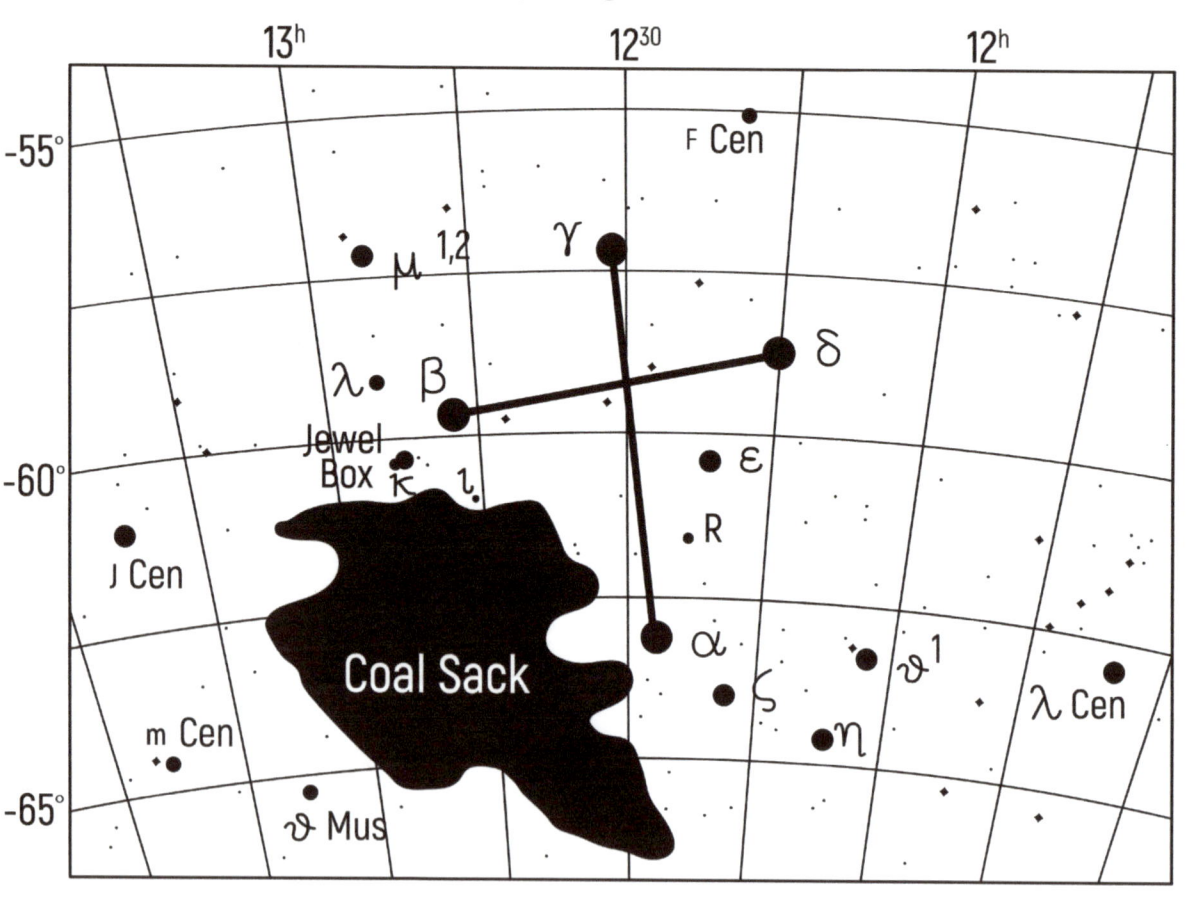

VIRGO THE VIRGIN

The "Virgin Mary" corresponds to the constellation Virgo, also known as Virgo the Virgin. The Latin term "Virgo" means virgin, and this virgin is also associated with the "house of bread", which translates to Bethlehem, a celestial location rather than an earthly one.

On December 25th, during the transition from the summer solstice back to the winter solstice, the days grow shorter and colder. From the perspective of the northern hemisphere, the Sun appears to move south, diminishing in size and intensity. This gradual shortening of days symbolises death.

By December 22nd, the Sun reaches its lowest point in the sky, seemingly pausing for three days, symbolising death. At this point, the Sun aligns with the Southern Cross, or the "crux", on December 22nd, 23rd, and 24th.

On the 25th, the Sun begins to move one degree north, heralding longer days, warmth, and the arrival of spring.

And so the story goes...

The Sun's symbolic journey, mirroring death and rebirth, parallels the movement of the Sun towards the north, heralding spring and salvation. The celebration of the Sun coincided with the spring equinox, known as "Easter", a time when days grew longer and brighter, signifying new life.

SUN AND SON

Hence, the parallels drawn between Jesus, considered the Son of God, and the Sun are profound. Jesus' travels with his twelve disciples mirror the Sun's journey through the twelve constellations. The association between Jesus and the zodiac dates back to the 11th century.

12 CONSTELLATIONS

The prevalence of the number twelve in the Bible further reinforces this allegorical interpretation:

- 12 Disciples
- 12 tribes of Israel
- 12 Brothers of Joseph
- 12 Great Patriarchs
- 12 Old Testament Prophets
- 12 Kings of Israel
- 12 Princes of Israel
- Jesus at the temple at the age of 12
- 12 hours of the day
- 12 hours of night

As is noted in Galatians, *"which things are an allegory; for these are the two covenants; the one from the mount Sinai, which gendereth to bondage, which is Agar"*.

"For this Agar is Mount Sinai in Arabia, and answereth to Jerusalem which now is, and is in bondage with her children."

Galatians 4: 24-25 (KJV)

WHOSE CROSS?

The Cross of the Zodiac, also known as the life of the Sun, holds significant spiritual symbolism. However, it has been misappropriated to represent what some term as "pagan Christianity".

THE COUNCIL OF CHALCEDON 451 A.D
ECUMENICAL COUNCIL OF THE ROMAN CATHOLIC CHURCH

"This wise and saving creed, the gift of divine grace, was sufficient for a perfect religion. For its teaching about the Father, Son, and Holy Spirit is complete, and it sets out the Lord's becoming human to those who faithfully accept it. Since we—the Catholic bishops—have formulated these things with all possible accuracy and attention, the sacred and universal synod decrees that no one is permitted to produce, or even write down or compose any other creed or to think or teach otherwise.

As for those who dare either to compose another creed, or promulgate, or teach or hand down another creed for those who wish to convert to a recognition of the truth from Hellenism or from Judaism, or from any kind of heresy at all, if they be bishops or clerics, the bishops are to be deposed from the episcopacy and the clerics from the clergy; if they be monks or lay folks, they are to be anathematized. Anathema means a thing devoted to God without hope of being redeemed. If an animal is to be slain, therefore, a thing or person doomed to destruction: a curse, a man or woman accursed, devoted to the direst of woes. (1st Corinthians 16:22) "If any man loves not the Lord Jesus Christ, let him be anathematized."

They used and continue to use Christianity. It's just that Black people don't believe it; they still hold onto the slave-master's fictitious myths and lies.

African Bondage

"To win a people for Christ, it is necessary to Europeanize them. Behind all systems of administration lies the fundamental question of what we intend to make of the African. This question has, whether in explicit terms or not, been answered in several ways. One possible and largely practiced policy is that of repression, which means keeping the native – Afrikan –in a subjected and inferior position, keeping him in his own place as a mere serf-slave of the dominant race."

The Golden Stool by Edwin W. Smith, Page 173

The Bible

In Latin: Biblia Sacra Vulgate

or

The Sun Book

The Bible is an Astrotheological Literary Hybrid.

Colonialism

"The first method begins by destroying the institutions, traditions, religion, and habits of the people and then superimposes upon the ruins whatever the governing power considers to be a better administration system. The other method, while checking the worst abuses, tries to graft our highest civilization onto the soundly-rooted native stock, bringing out the best of what is in the native tradition and moulding it into a form consonant with our modern ideas and higher standards."

Golden Stool - Page 186

The Sun of God

"The Christian religion is a parody on the worship of The Sun, in which they call Christ Jesus in place of the Sun, and pay him the same adoration which was originally paid to the Sun."

The Theological Works of Thomas Paine, p. 283.

Images of Jesus are always shown with the sun disk or halo behind his head.

In depictions of Jesus, the sun disk or halo behind his head is a recurring motif. Jesus' image is often superimposed over the centre of the Sun, akin to how ancient people revered and acknowledged the Sun's power.

The Sun of God comes every morning with a crown of thorns or sun rays illuminated in the background:

It is believed that the Sun of God arrives each morning with a crown of thorns, symbolised by sun rays. This Sun is also known as the light of the world and the saviour of mankind.

CROWN OF THORNS

TIME AND AGE

Several Bible scriptures allude to the concept of "The Time" or "The Age", including:

- ⌘ Matthew 28.20
- ⌘ Matthew 12.32
- ⌘ Matthew 13.39
- ⌘ Matthew 24.3
- ⌘ Luke 18.30
- ⌘ Corinthians 3
- ⌘ Corinthians 10
- ⌘ Ephesians 1
- ⌘ Ephesians 12
- ⌘ Hebrews 9
- ⌘ Job 8.8
- ⌘ Revelation 15

PERIOD IN TIME

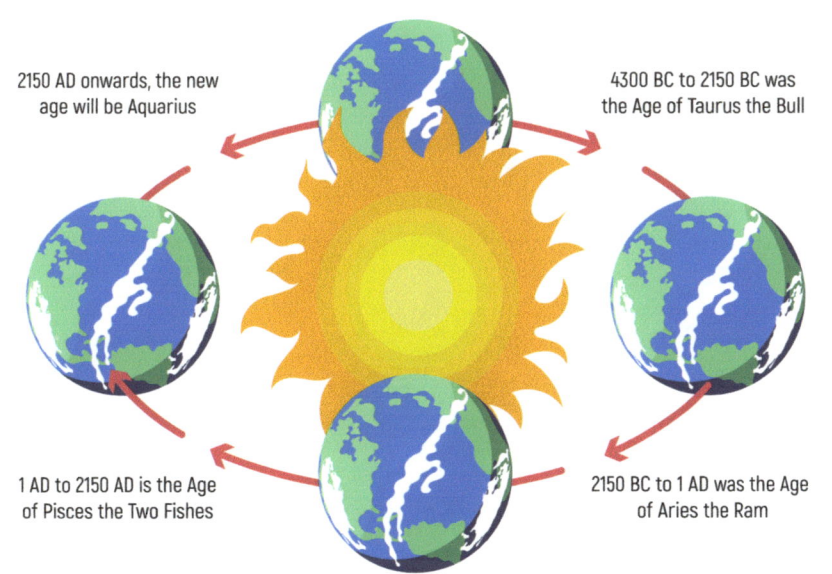

The concept of "The Age" represents distinct periods in time, each lasting precisely 2150 years. This idea is rooted in the procession of the equinoxes, a cycle taking 26,000 years to complete, known as the "Great Age".

Here are the ages as described:

- From 4300 BC to 2150 BC was the Age of Taurus the Bull.
- From 2150 BC to 1 AD was the Age of Aries the Ram.
- From 1 AD to 2150 AD is the Age of Pisces the Two Fishes.
- From 2150 AD onwards, the new age will be Aquarius.

VERNAL EQUINOX

AGES OF THE BULL, AGE OF THE RAM

THE AGE OF THE TWO FISHES AND AQUARIUS

MOSES = THE AGE OF ARIES (2150 BC - 1 AD)

The Bible references three "Ages" while alluding to a fourth. In the Old Testament, Moses descends from the mountain to find the people worshipping a Golden Calf, leading to his anger and the breaking of the commandments, as recounted in Exodus 32. However, it is important to consider the historical context:

- ⌘ The name Moses originates from the Egyptian story of Thutmose III.
- ⌘ In the Old Testament, Moses comes down the mountain with the Ten Commandments, symbolizing the end of the Age of Taurus the Bull and the idol worship of the Golden Calf.
- ⌘ This signifies the beginning of a new age of Aries, hence the blowing of the Rams' horn by the Jews.
- ⌘ Jesus symbolises the Age of Pisces, the Two Fishes, starting in 1 AD (with Jesus' supposed birth in 4 BC).
- ⌘ Luke 28.20: "Teaching them to observe all things that I have commanded you, and lo, I am with you always, even to the end of the Age/Aeon."
- ⌘ This leads us to the Age of Aquarius, the Water Bearer, from 2150 AD to 4300 AD, associated with the New World Order.

Thutmose 111

JESUS = THE AGE OF PISCES (1 AD - 2150 AD)

LAW GIVERS THROUGH THE AGES

- Manu is the lawgiver in India.
- Minos is the lawgiver of Crete.
- Thothma is the lawgiver of Egypt.
- Moses follows as the lawgiver for Christianity in Egypt.
- Sakaya-Budda in East India.
- Abram-Abraham, the Hebrew or Iz'zerlite lawgiver.
- Zarathustra-Zoroaster, the Persian lawgiver.
- KA'YU-Confucius in China.
- Sargon of Akkad (2250 BC).

MANU, LAW-GIVER OF INDIA

MINOS, LAW-GIVER OF CRETE

MISES, LAW-GIVER OF SYRIA

Sacrifices are made to symbolise the ushering of a New Age

In essence, various religions mark the transition from one age to another, symbolising the shedding of the old age through sacrifices and rituals.

Jesus ushers in the Age of Pisces, symbolised by the "Two Fishes". Biblical references support this transition, such as the story of Jesus feeding the multitude of 5000.

Additionally:

- By the Sea of Galilee, Jesus calls two brothers who were fishermen.
- The fish symbol, rooted in pagan astrology, aligns with Jesus starting his earthly ministry at the age of twelve in the Age of Pisces (1 AD).
- Jesus' supposed birthday is in 4 AD.
- In the Passover story, the man carrying the pitcher of water symbolises the sun sign Aquarius, the water bearer. Jesus refers to the Age of Aquarius following the Age of Pisces.
- Jesus' references to the 'End Times' in Matthew 28:20 coincide with the end of the Age of Pisces and the beginning of the New Age, Aquarius.

Many biblical stories can be traced back to the Temple of Luxor in Kemet/Egypt, with its walls serving as living proof of the 'Miracle Birth' 15 centuries before the advent of Christianity. These narratives are rooted in the story of HORUS. The tale of Noah, dating back to 2600 BC, is recorded as "The Epic of Gilgamesh".

SACRIFICED/CRUCIFIED

The Council of Nicaea 325 A.D

"The First Ecumenical Council of the Christian church, convened in ancient Nicaea, was called by the Emperor Constantine, an unbaptized catechumen or neophyte, who presided over the opening session and took part in the discussions. He hoped that a general council of the church would solve the problem created in the Eastern church by Arianism, a heresy first proposed by Arius of Alexandria, which affirmed that Christ is not divine but a created being.

"I [Pope Sylvester] did not attend the council but was represented by legates. The council condemned Arius and, with reluctance on the part of some, incorporated the nonscriptural word 'homoousios' (of one substance) into a creed (the Nicene Creed) to signify the absolute equality of the Son with the Father.

"The Emperor then exiled Arius, an act that, while manifesting a solidarity of church and state, underscored the importance of secular patronage in ecclesiastical affairs."

— The Encyclopedia Britannica

The Council of Nicaea 325 A.D

HORUS = JESUS

SON WORSHIP OR SUN WORSHIP

ALMIGHTY POWER

SEEK TRUTH IF YOU DARE

HISTORIANS

Most Historians at the time or after the time of Jesus didn't write accounts that have been able to authenticate his life and works:

- Autus Perseus (60 AD)
- Columella (1st Cent – AD)
- Dio Chrysostom (C. 40 – C. 112 AD)
- Justus of Tiberius (C. 80 AD)
- Livy (59 BC – 17 AD)
- Lucanus (63 AD)
- Phlegon (1st. Cent. AD)
- Pomponius Mela (40 AD)
- Petronius (D. 66 AD)
- Lucius Florus (1st.-2nd . Cent. AD)
- Rufus Curtius (1st. Cent. AD)
- Quintilian (C. 35-C. 100 AD)
- Seneca (4 BC? -65 AD)
- Valerius Maximus (C. 20 AD)

FLAVIUS JOSEPHUS

"About this time there lived Jesus, a wise man, if indeed one ought to call him a man. For he was one who performed surprising deeds and was a teacher of such people as accept the truth gladly. He won over many Jews and many of the Greeks. He was the Messiah. And when, upon the accusation of the principal men among us, Pilate had condemned him to a cross, those who had first come to love him did not cease. He appeared to them spending a third day restored to life, for the prophets of God had foretold these things and a thousand other marvels about him. And the tribe of Christians, so called after him, has still to this day not disappeared."

(Confirmed to be a fake)

Ancient Egypt: the original Blueprint of:

- Baptism
- Afterlife
- Judgment
- Virgin Birth
- Resurrection
- Crucifixion
- Ark of the Covenant

- Communion
- The Great Flood
- Easter
- Christmas
- Passover
- Saviour

Records show that from 1967 to 1982, Israelis underwent an intensive search of the Sinai Desert for evidence that 2 million people roamed there for 40 years, but no evidence has been found or has been found to date. Apparently, there is also no account of an Exodus in Egypt.

Lawrence H. Schiffman, president of Jewish studies at Usheba University, states:

"We cannot, in an academic way, determine whether these events happened; it is simply a matter of religious belief, as there is no historical proof of these events."

This is a collection of authors for further research:

- Ashra Kwesi
- Dr. Ben Jochannan
- Dick Gregory
- Delbert Blair
- Dr. Phil Valentine
- Dr. Llaila Afrika
- Ras Ben
- Dr. John Henrik Clarke
- Dr. Joy DeGruy
- Tony Browder
- Ivan Van Sertima
- Amos N. Wilson
- Chancellor Williams
- Cheikh Anta Diop
- Frances Cress Welsing
- John G. Jackson
- Dr. Runoko Rashidi
- Abdullah Bey
- Prof. James Smalls

www.ingramcontent.com/pod-product-compliance
Lightning Source LLC
Chambersburg PA
CBHW050854010526
44118CB00004BA/166